HOW TO BE A

Pink Flamingo

IN A
BROWN DUCK
POND

PAINTING THE SKY

BY LYNN LARSON ARMSTRONG

 **FriesenPress**

Suite 300 – 990 Fort Street
Victoria, BC, Canada V8V 3K2
www.friesenpress.com

Edited by
Florentia Scott and Felechia Brodie

Special thanks to Amber Hack Moon | Facebook "the jetstar design" for cover design and to Greg Huszar Photography.

ISBN
978-1-4602-0567-9 (Hardcover)
978-1-4602-0565-5 (Paperback)
978-1-4602-0566-2 (eBook)

1. Business & Economics, Entrepreneurship

Distributed to the trade by The Ingram Book Company

Table of Contents

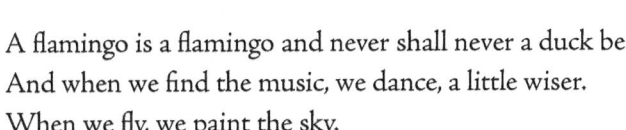

A flamingo is a flamingo and never shall never a duck be.
And when we find the music, we dance, a little wiser.
When we fly, we paint the sky.

This is dedicated to those who are ready to fly.

Introduction

Who do I think I am?

My name is Lynn Armstrong. I am dedicated to living well, and inspiring a revolution of living in colour.

I am a mother to two beautiful women, married for 33 years, a daughter, grandmother, and friend.

My guiding mantra is "do good things and good things happen." I am active in the community as a yoga teacher, fitness instructor and board member for a non-profit foundation.

I am an entrepreneur. In June 2011, I created Lynear Thinking to offer 20 years of expertise in corporate strategy, governance and communications to private sector companies, entrepreneurs and non-profits.

In 2012, I became the owner and publisher of SKY Magazine, and in 2013, I formed SKY Publishers Ltd., sharing the stories of entrepreneurs who paint the sky and live inspiring lives. In 2013, Myskymag.com took flight, reaching out to the world.

I live in my own vision, and I help people to live and work in theirs.

I am but one of the many voices, a conduit in this human experience who uses words so others may read this, and say, "me too."

And I do a mean chaturanga, baby.

That's who I think I am.

My Journey Begins with the Wind

I can't say for sure when it started. I think it may be somewhere between the time the wind was created and this very moment. For me, this quest for connection to the bigger idea is as natural as breathing. It always has been.

I have always felt there was something else. Something yet to be discovered. A bigger thing than just me. And that's pretty big, because I am a pretty big deal, according to my grandmother.

When I was a child, my grandmother said that I would be a nun when I grew up. I was terrified. I thought that the hand of God would reach down and grab me. So, of course, I did everything possible to avoid being on the list, including trading my brother quarters for dimes and blaming my big sister for things that I did, both of which worked because I was kind of . . . angelic.

While I was spared the hand of God as a child, I remain convinced there is some essence bigger than me. Something bigger than all of us. This "something" that I believe exists connects us to each other in a way that defines our humanity and the legacy that we are creating together.

I believe the answer to the question, "Who am I" is the answer to all things, for to know "myself" is to know what I have to give.

And so my quest has been to find my way back to the answer to this question, "Who am I?" and that brings me to my yogic journey.

In my quest to understand the answer to this question, I have discovered that this answer - this gift - is hidden by layers of titles and roles, each one essentially a job description, a temporary description of what I do, not who I am.

Over time, I have compromised for money, status and what I believed my family needed to be secure. I did my best to fit in and prove myself in the world, with success measured by the zeros in my pay cheque and the title on my business card.

I have discovered the temporary nature of these titles, and the vulnerability to which I exposed myself when I could no longer continue to compromise. The day I said "no more" and backed out of my parking stall was the day I began to find the gifts that were buried deep within my exterior that would carry me through and out. I call that day my day of emancipation. It truly was the beginning of a journey to freedom.

Words have been my salvation for as long as I can remember, as it was for my grandmother who saw something in me that was terrifying to me. I am a writer. I write to understand and to offer a perspective on what it all means. I also write to remember what I have learned, so that I would know better and do better should a second chance come my way.

Since 2011, I have been on a personal journey to redefine my life, my work and contribution to this world, and to find a community that would accept me as I am: a high-heel wearing, sequin loving fashionista with a head for business, strategy and a penchant for beautiful words and stories.

As a result, I did find my "edge" as we say in yoga. (the "edge" is a precipice – a precarious, ledge hanging, life pondering state where you are challenged to find a way to persevere and move beyond it, or submit and fall). On that day, I fell from the sky and began to fade to white.

At the precipice, I did not submit and go away never to be heard from again. Instead I fought my way back to freedom.

Freedom on paper is not freedom. I was not free from that secret or the pain. I had been hurt badly. I resolved to write my way though the anger to understand it and to find a way out of that situation that hurt me so badly.

I decided to write about the day I fell from the sky and began to fade to white, and how I learned to fly again.

The words flowed like water off a duck's back. But it was all the bad water. I knew I had to rethink my intention because I did not want to live through that experience over and over again.

I wrote 22 drafts of the text in the 3rd person in an effort to distance myself from the story and create a safe environment for me to tell this story. On the 23rd draft, I switched to the first person.

Another three drafts followed as I struggled to find a way to share my story.

Throughout this journey, my yoga and writing practice provided me with the tools to find the balance between holding on and letting go, between the past, the present and the future, and living in awareness.

The process of writing the book was indeed the light that kept me moving forward, restoring my voice and helping me to understand my fear.

My writing process ran parallel to attempts to rebuild my professional life.

I set out to locate the person whom I was yet to be, and in the course of that journey, found my way back to the place that I had always intended to be some day.

Flamingos and Ducks

When we think of the flamingo, we think of bright colours. Duck is a strong untwilled linen or cotton fabric, used for casual or work clothes and sails.

The brown duck is often associated with predictable, guarded, serious and safe behaviour. The flamingo is gregarious, fabulous, fiery and flamboyant.

The flamingo celebrates and dances; the brown duck perches and waddles.

Flamingos like to party in mobs. We have all seen the ever-so-popular lawn flamingos that converge in packs of 40 or 50. Brown ducks tend to prefer the linear approach to moving together.

Flamingos are revered for their beauty and brown ducks for their nobility.

Flamingos are celebrated *objet's d'art*, and ducks appear most commonly on mantles, in studies, boardrooms and hunting shacks.

A well-fed, healthy flamingo is more vibrantly coloured and thus a more desirable mate. A white or pale flamingo, however, is usually unhealthy or malnourished. Captive flamingos are a notable exception; many turn a pale pink as they are not fed carotene at levels comparable to the wild.[1]

Flamingos tend to live in regions that have very little food to offer other animals. As a result, they benefit from not having natural predators. Their predators are a variety of other large birds. Vultures and storks can swoop in and take the young to consume them in an instant. There is nothing that can be done but try to keep the young close enough to the adults to ward off predatory birds.

---

1 http://www.seaworld.org/animal-info/info-books/flamingo/behavior.htm

The flamingo has only one line of defense and that is their very powerful legs. If flamingos can find out about the predator soon enough, they will be able to fly away. When flamingos fly, they paint the sky.

About this story

Today, I heard quacking, but then I realized I was just listening in the wrong language. Since 2010, I have been observing the fowl world and more specifically communication, adaptation and behavioral strategies.

I am such a pink flamingo. I worked in the brown duck pond for over 20 successful and rewarding years as a corporate planner, strategist and communicator. I have worked with some of the brightest minds, helping them to forge new directions and bringing those futures to life.

I became interested in the contrast between the flamingo and the brown duck because I find these feathered friends to be very similar to our own species in the world of work and life. The basic premise of "How to Be a Pink Flamingo in a Brown Duck Pond" is one of understanding and celebrating the unique qualities the different birds of a feather bring to the life and work experience.

The concept was originally introduced in May 2010 by yours truly in a blog post entitled, "How to be a Pink Flamingo in a Brown Duck Pond". As of May 2012, the post had exceeded 7,000 page views.

People ask me, "am I a flamingo or a duck?" The answer is, yes and no. They are you and me: people who think and work conceptually and people who think and work in a linear fashion. The point is not to define and enclose oneself in a given identity, in fact, quite the opposite. We are all birds of a feather, regardless of whether we weigh more heavily on the pink or brown side. There are distinctions and unique qualities that are there when you know where to look.

How to be a Pink Flamingo in a Brown Duck Pond is about finding the courage to stand up and stand out, learn to fly and change the colour of the sky. These are the chapters of my journey. I offer these experiences and observations to those who are ready to fly.

CHAPTER 1:
Finding Nirvana

$50,000 in 5 years or bust

At the age of 30, I had done everything I never wanted to do again, from being a receptionist and secretary to commission sales.

As a goal oriented person, when I do something I usually create a solid plan that ensures I follow through. I registered for University, taking a student loan because I knew I would never quit until I accomplished my goal of graduating with a degree. My daughters were two and four years old; we had a small bungalow that cost $428.00 a month (taxes included) and a car. I drove a school bus to make the car payment and pay for dance lessons, shoes and clothes for my daughters.

I attended full time classes and raised my children, running them to and from school. I drove a school bus in the morning and afternoon, and did homework from 8:00 PM to 3:00 AM every day. Journalism school was intense with classes all day and assignments in every medium, including print, magazine, radio, television and documentary with some law and ethics thrown in there for good measure. I used to say, if I can survive for three months, I will be okay. I said that for five years, and we did survive, as a family, on approximately $10,000 a year.

During that time, my husband returned to university as well to study Engineering, after the economy went south in our neck of the woods. We figured if we were going to be poor, we may as well do it when the children were too young to know the difference. I sewed my daughters` clothes all summer with my friend Michelle. Each year, as we fought for student loans and funding, I began to understand the value of having writing skills.

I graduated from the University of Regina with a Bachelor of Arts in 1995, and a Bachelor of Arts in Journalism and Communication in 1996, with $60,000 in debt, a family to raise, house payments and the hope of making my living as a writer, inspired by John Lennon, Janis Joplin, Neil Young, Johnny Cash, William Shakespeare and my grandmother, Anne Larson.

I have always had a penchant for art, fashion, décor, writing, rocks stars and poets. I chose to pursue a career in journalism because it could include all the things I love, and it seemed to be the most practical approach, since it would be difficult to make my living as a poet and I can`t really carry a tune. Or at least I shouldn't in public.

I hoped to make a living as a reporter, or failing that, I could join the "dark side" of communications, as it was called in J-School. (I thought of it more as the "dimly lit side".)

Sitting on the stage during convocation, I started thinking about the next five years. I had a family to support. My husband was still in university and I had two small children. How was I going to turn this degree into a house payment, shoes and dance lessons?

It occurred to me on that stage at convocation that I had no idea what I was good at, and I couldn`t think of a grand career goal, like becoming a great novelist or the evening anchor on the national news. Those were dreams that I could not afford because real life was waiting for me. I had to make a living, pure and simple, so I set a monetary goal for myself.

There on the stage, waiting for my name to be called, I set a goal to make $50,000 in the next five years.

The Dimly Lit Side

I got my first corporate job at a federal crown corporation where I worked Monday to Friday in the Communications department. I was hired on a work term for about $24,000 a year, which was a considerable improvement on all fronts from driving a school bus.

I was also fortunate to land a job as a weekend reporter for the local newspaper where I worked Friday to Monday writing whatever came my way. I love journalism and I always said I would do it for free. That was closer to the truth than one would expect. My weekend reporting gig didn't really pay the bills and it eventually ended when the shift changed, interfering with my Monday to

Friday job on the dimly-lit side in communications. I picked up some freelance writing assignments whenever I could to keep my journalistic skills sharp.

Raising a family was my first priority, so I was grateful for the corporate communications job. It was there that I developed a love and appreciation for strategy, good leaders and a culture that enabled people to be their best.

I was completely in awe of the environment and my leaders, many of whom continue to be my mentors today. I gratefully and enthusiastically soaked up all that this environment had to teach me. I loved my job. It would become the bar against which I have measured every work experience thus far.

My journalism skills and the fact that I was anxious to work and learn helped me to make a dent in the corporate reporting world.

I asked for the opportunity to write the annual report. At the time, I knew nothing about writing annual reports. All I knew was that everyone else seemed to dread the job, so that created an opportunity for me.

I researched annual reports, ordering every annual report written in Canada. I read each one of them, looking for the elements that would make a great annual report, aside from the obligatory CEO message, Management Discussion and Analysis (MD&A), Strategic Plan and Results, Financials and Governance. To me, annual reports are historic documents that tell the story of the organization. Its audience is its owners, employees, and the general public. Annual reports are also about public accountability. I wanted to change the way we read annual reports.

I decided to go back to what I knew, which was how to tell a story. I set up interviews with the top agricultural producers in Canada and shared their stories in the annual report. I became known in some circles as the *Annual Report Queen* because the reports won awards. My first annual report won awards. I went on to write the Annual Report for two more award-winning years.

Writing annual reports was interesting and exciting for me. Not only did I love the competitive challenge, I was able to bring the art of storytelling into the corporate realm.

Writing annual reports taught me about project management, people management, and the value of good organizational planning. In the course of writing annual reports, I ended up reconstructing the corporate plan in such a way that it could be reported upon in a succinct format. I created a one page business plan format that included a balanced scorecard inspired model outlining strategic objectives, measures, targets, initiatives and results.

After three years in Communications, I was asked to join the Policy and Planning Division, facilitating the creation of the Corporate Plan. I was able to bring the structure of balanced scorecard thinking to the planning process and into the reporting processes. Those Corporate Plans also received awards for two out of three years.

In the course of writing annual reports and corporate plans, I learned something valuable about business, leadership and communication. First, when things are going well, shout it from the roof top. When they are not going well, shout it from the roof top.

Being so close to the decision making process was exciting for me as an employee, as I could see how I was contributing to the corporation. I thought that if everyone could see what I saw, they would be excited and inspired, and have a clear line of sight between themselves and the work of the corporation.

I wanted people to see the business plan as I did, so I began creating processes that would bring the plan closer to the people, implementing the one page business plan as a communication piece, and moving the planning process deeper into the operations of the organization where the people actually do the work.

My goal was to create clarity of vision and what it means to "me" (the person who comes to work everyday) and to help leaders create alignment of resources and focus on the right things. The possibility of connecting with one person at a time became my mantra in creating business plans and inspired the creation of my vision for *Lynear Thinking* in 1996.

P.S. In five years, I reached my goal of $50K, and then some.

Blue Skies, Nothing but Blue Skies

The colour of the sky in my world is decidedly blue, and it always has been. I believe in possibility, the power of vision, doing good things and the importance of focusing on the right things to make it happen.

I was invited to give a blue sky presentation at a corporate meeting. I decided to share my vision of the perfect job wearing black leather pants.

Lynn Larson Armstrong

The room was filled with members of our department, as well as the executive. The first PowerPoint slide in black with white letter appeared, "Lynear Thinking." The song, "It's my life", by Bon Jovi began to blast.

This ain't a song for the broken-hearted
No silent prayer for the faith-departed
I ain't gonna be just a face in the crowd
You're gonna hear my voice
When I shout it out loud

[Chorus:]
It's my life
It's now or never
I ain't gonna live forever
I just want to live while I'm alive
It's my life
My heart is like an open highway
Like Frankie said
I did it my way
I just wanna live while I'm alive
It's my life

My co-worker mouthed, "What are you doing?" I smiled back at her. This was my rooftop and I was shouting out my intention, although in retrospect, it might have seemed a bit like anarchy had broken out.

I shared a vision where each person is the CEO of his or her own life, where 'CEO' stands for 'creative, entrepreneurial and optimistic.' I said in this place, there would be no "no", only "how."

I said that vision came from the inspired, and not necessarily from the promoted. I envisioned a place where we would work with purpose, for purpose.

As the words flashed on the screen and the music blasted, the crowd was speechless. Some people sat with their arms crossed, others smiled, while others were afraid to smile.

Lynear Thinking: It's my life.

> Basic Tenets: Every person lives through purpose. Every day
> is about living a vision. Every moment counts.

Each person is the CEO of his / her own life: CEO = Creative, Optimistic, and Energetic.

Don't hold me back: Never say no to an idea. Ask how it can grow. The power to lead comes from vision. Yours. Mine. Ours. Vision is two way.

Vision is not necessarily for the sighted, or the promoted: Vision keeps you going when everything else tells you to stop. "Two years planning, a documentary movie, and this blind guy barely makes it to Camp 1?"

Inspirare. Breathe in and live. Oxygen deprivation does strange things to the human body. Heart rates go haywire, brain function decreases, blood thickens, and intestines shut down.

My Nirvana

I knew I had found the way ahead. My vision was clearly defined from that moment on. I didn't get fired, but then again, I never thought I would. I was not afraid. I had faith in my leaders that they would receive *Lynear Thinking* in the way that it was intended: to inspire creative thinking at work.

Every day after, I set out a path to be the best I could be. I worked at being the best writer I could be and I won awards. I wanted to became the best corporate planner I could be, so I studied, learned from the masters of Kaplan and Norton, Prahalad and Hamel. I was welcomed into the executive realm to be a part of climbing the corporate hill of what's next. It was the most awe-inspiring time of my career. I believed that I had struck Nirvana.

I moved to another pond (which felt like I was leaving home) to take on a management role and I loved every minute of that job as well. I was truly blessed in working with people who had a desire to get somewhere. It was so exciting to help them create plans, and continue my personal mission of bringing the plan and the people together.

I later expanded on this rendition of *Lynear Thinking* at a School of Business Leadership course in Queen's University. There I learned that being good, in fact great, at something is not enough. I learned that I am not enough by myself. That it takes a team.

I committed to finding out what makes a good leader and to be the best leader I could be. And then I worked at that. I took the courses. I read the books. I watched the masters, or at least who I thought they were. But mostly I listened, watched and paid attention to how people responded to the way they were being treated.

I found that if people are treated well, they will flourish, going to the end of the world and back again to do a good job. If not, they will hide in the weeds and hope for the best until a better job comes along.

The trick is for good people and good employers to find each other. Not all people make good employees, and not all employers are good. The greatest success of my career has been being a leader. I feel very grateful to those who have given me their dedication and talent during our time together. Even though we no longer work together, we continue to have a friendship that I value very much.

I made a 20 year career out of building strategic plans and business plans. To date I have moved about 200 board members and executives up a hill, gotten them to the end every single time, with a business plan in hand, and written countless words about what it all means. Over the years, I helped create futures and communicate it so that others could see it too, bringing elements of my own vision of *Lynear Thinking* to the process. From 50,000 feet right down to the ground where the work happens, I have seen first-hand the impact that work has on our lives, both as employees and owners.

Now I see Nirvana as a place where success is achieved through organizing, engaging and inspiring people who act like owners and not workers, who make the best use of resources and work effectively and efficiently, who treat customers like they are the most important people in the universe (because they are), and who represent the business in the community. There`s no mention of money, but that`s because I am a flamingo, and not a duck.

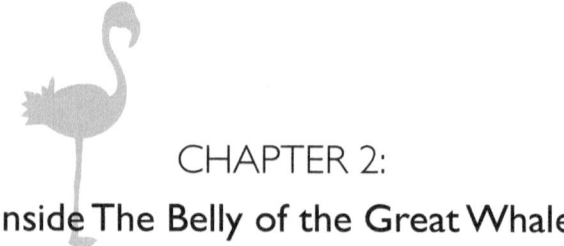

CHAPTER 2:

Inside The Belly of the Great Whale

Claustrophobia and the Big Fish

It was November 2006. I had just turned 45 a few days earlier. I was sitting at my computer, staring at a blank screen. I was at a point in my life when I realized that I needed to change something. Say something. Do something. But I had no voice. I was for the first time in my life speechless.

My job as a strategic planner had become all consuming. We had been swallowed whole, implementing mergers and joint ventures. There was no fun to be had inside the belly of the great whale. The environment was politically charged and the ducks were running the show, or they were hiding in the weeds hoping, as we all were, for the chaos to end. The flamingos were doing their best to keep up with the dance, but the orchestra was playing double time.

Efficiency and the bottom line was the all consuming strategy of the day. Money was counted daily, once, if not twice. Time was measured in hours and minutes. People were measured and rewarded for the doing the most with the least amount of time and money. As a planner, my job was to integrate the processes and help our team translate value to our owners. We did that by implementing a consulting model, which included agreements that were signed off by our owners as customers. But despite improvements, the work did not stop. I consistently worked 12-hour days six to seven days a week to keep up.

The irony is, during that time, I can honestly say our team worked together fantastically. We had to come together and we did. We made it palatable for each other. We laughed and joked about dedicating days of the week to use our powers for good or evil (Week 1: Good – Monday, Wednesday, Friday; Evil – Tuesday, Thursday. Week 2: Good – Tuesday, Thursday; Evil – Monday, Wednesday, Friday.) We had a "That was Easy" button that we would slam victoriously after we dealt with a difficult duck. We cried together on days when it got to be overwhelming, because that was the best we could do some days. Sometimes we'd break for 'black and delicious' at the local Irish pub. From our vantage point as a service area, we saw things. When things got tough, I used to say, "We need to keep our eye on our own ball and let whatever happens outside of our area happen."

On the personal front, my life was changing dramatically and so was I. My children were now young women, growing up into young adults. My love of writing had all but dissipated, as every word I wrote was no longer mine because it was what we called in Journalism, *spin*. I did not feel safe and the sense of connection to purpose was getting harder and harder to recognize. I was not finding joy in my work as I had before, and I knew the pace was not sustainable.

It was that day in November that I realized change was imminent, that I had been many things to many people, becoming the person that I needed to be, but not who I am. I realized that somewhere on the other side of this reality was another person whose potential was unknown to me. So I decided to change on purpose, with purpose.

Walking Against My Own Traffic

As a strategic planner, I naturally established my intention, a set of directions, and a deadline. I gave myself one year to change my mind, my body, and my job. I wanted to be in a different space in my career, as I was looking for advancement, challenge and a chance to make a dent in this world.

I pledged that I would work responsibly and stop being a hero by working 18 hours a day to get some of my life back. I said that I wanted to figure out what to fill my life with besides work. In the corporate world where I spent the majority of my time, I knew that changing direction would be no small feat because it must begin with changing minds. Every good and worthy planner knows that the way to change head space is to cause a disruption in the experience. Alter reality. To walk against the traffic, as it were.

To all novice change makers, this is no easy task. Invoking change can create a tidal wave of events that can challenge personal values, belief systems and create reactions that you never thought possible. Few corporate giants do this successfully.

Change must be managed, monitored and adjusted according to the experience and the outcomes.

So I used the same concepts of business to invoke a change in my life and headspace. I committed to four principles to guide my actions:

1. Choose defiance.

2. Listen and seek to understand.

3. Practice imperfection.

4. Avoid rooms with no doors.

Principle 1: Choose defiance

Reality is often defined by fears and insecurities that prevent us from doing things that we would like to do. We are afraid that if we take that step, we might fall into an abyss of nothingness and lose everything we have and know. We are afraid that we are not good enough.

We are afraid of failure; we are hardwired to believe that failure is . . . well, bad. In order to alter my reality I knew that I had to challenge my own assumptions about who I am, what I value, what I am about, and what I am capable of. So I made a commitment to defiance.

When I say that, eyebrows tend to rise. Defiance is natural. Birds defy gravity. Trees grow in rock. Babies are born, kicking and screaming. Defiance is a natural process of renewal and change. Without defiance, our earth would cease to revolve. The sun would not shine. And we would cease to exist. We have been raised and socialized to behave and so we have forgotten how to resist status quo.

Through our institutional behaviours, we can lose our ability to naturally change, grow, and resist status quo – or death, as I like to call it. Defiance is important to growth, because through defiance, we are forced to see another side. Explore a new possibility. Walk against the traffic.

I set a goal to commit three defiant acts that would challenge my personal fears, assumptions and insecurities, find my voice and ultimately my direction. Defiance meant saying no more often, not working late, not trying to impress people by over achieving. It meant eating the foods I like and living the way I want to live. It meant testing new boundaries, and taking the risk of falling, and learning how to land.

Defiance taught me to challenge my own personal status quo, and all the conventions and limitations that have influenced me in the past – as far back as my childhood and as deep down as my inner most fears and insecurities.

I likely committed more than three acts of defiance because there was a ripple effect. I tattooed an image on my lower back that symbolizes growth and balance. I pierced my nose, much to my mother's dismay, and I stepped into uncharted territory when it came to business and my personal life.

I changed everything, discarding those things that did not feel good. I changed my diet and committed to a fitness program. I stopped working long hours. I became stronger and healthier. When I realized that clear sunny days were not in the forecast, I chose happiness and another pond.

I learned along the way, and discovered that I have the power to choose my destiny as we all do. I discovered that exercising the power to choose destiny is more difficult than letting life happen to you.

Today, a sign in my office says, *Commit 3 Acts of Defiance a Day*. Defiance helped me to discover the courage and strength that I needed to grow, and it helped me to rediscover my values, which continue to carry me forward.

Principle 2 - Listen and seek to understand

We hold ourselves back with what we tell ourselves about ourselves. These thoughts betray our potential. In fact, we are only able to accomplish what we can ourselves imagine.

What we think about is who we are. What we imagine, is what we become. So in order to liberate my thinking, I committed to listening to my own self talk to hear what I was thinking about, so that I would be able to understand better who I came to be, who I am, and who I have yet to be.

Listening, I discovered, is an art from. And listening to oneself takes discipline. It requires the ability to block out the personal noise that we have going on in our heads all the time. To develop listening skills, I learned to play the guitar, since I have always had a penchant for rock stars.

I also practiced yoga to find ways to balance my energy, quiet my thinking and to learn to breathe. Yoga also helped me to step back from my classic habit of multitasking because it demands a focused mind. (I discovered that while standing on my head, for instance, I could not think multiple thoughts or I would fall over.)

I set a personal goal to "seek to understand" rather than jumping to conclusions and reacting to my environment. This too took some practice. I needed to learn to listen to what was being said rather than letting judgments fly, thereby limiting the potential of the moment.

What I was thinking about, observing, feeling, worrying about or wondering about became the subject of my writing. Every night, I would sit down at my computer, close my eyes, and look into the darkness with my fingers resting on my keyboard. I would reflect on the day and events, how I was feeling, and why. I committed to be positive in my reactions, but insightful in my quest to understand my thinking process, not judge.

The writing process took on a life of its own from there, as an art, not a science. It reached those places in the mind and soul that were rarely visited. When I wrote, I focused on the sound of my own heart beating, and the cadence of my breath. The words and stories fell from my fingertips to reveal whatever was there at that moment in time.

I had written poetry before, but this was different because it was not my intention to create poetry. It was my intention to journey through words to see what they would say.

The first poem in this collection, "Write me Away" established the intention to be free and to explore, to give way to the flood of images that, when translated into words, would embody a poetic heartbeat and pulse.

Principle 3 - Practice imperfection

Perfectionism breeds fear and insecurity. I am a recovering perfectionist. In the writing process, I made a commitment to let go of each poem without revising, editing and perfecting.

After every poem, I saved it, named it and closed the file. Each poem took anywhere from three minutes to 30 minutes to write. They are what they were at that moment in time. And they remain, with minor editing for punctuation and capitalization (so as not to offend the English majors in the crowd.)

After some time, I went back to the file and discovered that there were over 30 poems that I had written over a period of approximately five months. I read them and realized that a change was occurring in three stages as revealed by the themes. I sorted the poems under the titles Emerging, Defiant and Breaking Through.

In my reflection, I knew that I still had a distance to travel, and that I would never really get there. I also took notice of the recurring nature imagery in the poems.

There is an ebb and flow of time and the fact that our coexistence together cannot be accidental, that we are connected to the sky, the rocks, birds, trees, the oceans and to each other.

The interesting thing about being human is that our potential is far beyond that of our natural life / body form. Maybe that is the way it is intended to be. Maybe as an individual, we really are part of a larger story, and the part we play is but a sentence in the story of time.

Principle 4 - Avoid rooms with no doors

While in the midst of this self induced change, the merger that we had all given many days and nights to suffered under the weight of forces beyond our control. I had begun to increase overtime again. I was pushing back and speaking up about what was happening.

I found myself alone and exhausted, with no one to confide in. One day stands out in my mind. I was driving home, feeling like I was in a room with no doors. I felt trapped and frustrated. I tried calling friends and family, but no one was available. I needed to ground myself. That night, I picked up the phone to contact one of my mentors.

Through the course of our conversation, I came to the realization that I could not undergo this change alone. I needed help. I needed someone to be honest with me. So I asked if she knew of anyone who could coach me, and she said that she was available. The door opened up at that moment. It turns out the door is wherever we want it to be. We can and do open our own doors.

The door for me is to open the mind to the experience of others, to learn from each moment and each interaction and to listen as if I am about to learn the secrets of the universe. My coach and mentor held a mirror up to me, so that I could see myself honestly and confront those things that were holding me back from making the changes I need to make: fear of failure; judgment of self and others; and reacting to a damaged ego.

I took the steps to consider my next growth path, looking out longer term to realize long term goals. She helped me with tools and most importantly, she helped me to find my own door when I feel trapped and helpless.

The Result: Died of A . .

As a result of this journey, a collection of poetry emerged telling the stories of a collective life lived. The poems are a reflection of experiences, observations and memories of people and events. It is an accident of poetry, found walking against the traffic, told in the first person in 30 minutes or less. The final entry, "Message in a Bottle" is the only poem written outside of this process, as it was written with the intention to bring closure to the work.

Died of a . . .

An accident of poetry, found walking against the traffic, told in the first person, in 30 minutes or less.

Part 1: Emerging

Write me away

Write me away

Through the pain
Through the darkness
Write me away through the sadness
Through the disappointment
Through my life.

Write me away

Help me find the words that free my heart
That give me strength, courage and hope
Let me find my words so I can say them
Out loud
So others will hear me
And say them too.

Write me away

To another place that is safe
To say those words: I love you.

To a place where
Everything's alright

Write me away

Where no matter what I do
I am forgiven.
Write me away for not being strong
For not being good enough
For not being brave.

Write me away

For disappointing you
For letting you down
Write me away for just wanting to feel
To know that I'm still alive
Write me away
Where it's ok.

Emerging

A year from now
I will be different
Emerging from a place
Where I had to be
And become who I am
I will be able to see me
For all that I am
To look in the mirror
And see a person who is not afraid, confident
A person who is inspiring and worthwhile
A person who gives to others what they need to get through the day
A person who brings success to others
A person who has made mistakes
A person who forgives
And does not judge

Lynn Larson Armstrong

When others falter
A person who makes a difference in the world
A person who is worthwhile.
A year from now
I will break through the surface
Of my fears and securities
I will embrace my mistakes for the lessons that I have learned
I will embrace all that I am and all that I have
To find the other side of where I am
To discover what's left to be lived
To discover who I am and what I could be
A year from now I will be born.

45

When they look at me
They see someone else
Someone's mother,
Someone's wife
Someone's something.

I know my freedom is near
Deep down inside me
But so far away
So distant that I can't touch it
Can see it
Don't know what it looks like

I am alone in this journey
Because everyone has something to gain
By my staying the same.
Everyone has a stake
In my never changing.
The courage that it would take to let go
To free fall

To land wherever
And to pick up and go on

As I look out on my life
I don't know what is out there now
I just know that I feel trapped
On the other side of my life
Where lives my potential, my voice.
Needing to be heard.
But not knowing what to say.
Needing to be seen
But afraid to be revealed
Needing to be free
But chained
When is it ok to let go
To be free

What if letting go
Means losing everything
That I have and know
What if letting go
Means starting over

What if letting go means not being the kind of wife that I used to be
Not being the kind of mother they need me to be
Not being the kind of whatever it was that I was supposed to be
Stretch marks and scars I have paid my dues
Tracks of my life etched in my skin
I have earned the right to be beautiful
To feel free
To have a voice
To be desired
To be loved
To dance
To live
I am 45.

Lynn Larson Armstrong

Things I Think

All that I believed in
All that I am
All that I know
All that I feel
All that I am
So tired
Eyes fall
Breath slows
Drifting
Reading
Listening to me
My thoughts
Things I think

Nothing Profound

Sometimes I stare at my screen
My fingers on my key board
I wait for some words
To emerge
Something profound
That's never been said
Something that will right all the wrongs
And create some great insight.
Waiting.
For words.
Something.
Amazing.
Awakening.

Doors

There's a crack, that's how the light gets in,
The light lets you know there's still room to enter
Room in your heart, room in someone's life
Room for a chance.
The one you love waits for you
Don't let it close.
The door can separate you from your life.
Forever.
The door never opens to the same two people twice.

I . . . In the First person

I am at the edge of something.
I can feel it.
I am at the edge
I know not what is on the other side
I want to take a step but
I am afraid that I will fall
Indefinitely.
I am afraid to step forward but
I am afraid that if I don't
I will never know what's on the other side
I need to know, but
I am searching.
I must find it.
Me.

Imagine

Imagine all that could have been
Should have been
Would have been
If only I could have been more
Done more, seen more

Imagine all that could have be learned
If only I listened, heard, felt, cared

Imagine all the mistakes I could take back
If only I could see to the end of today
How my words affect you
How my attitudes shape yours

Imagine who I could have been
If only I could live in reverse
Turned left instead of right
Tried to understand and not reject your feelings

Imagine how much richer I could be
If only I had listened, cared, loved
Been less afraid of you,
Of myself, of letting go
Of trusting and being trusted.

I Am ...

Not a painter, nor a sculptor or musician
I can't carry a tune, I love to dance, but I lack grace
I love to write, but the words are locked inside of me
Leaving me with random thoughts of nothingness
Rambling, searching for the rhythm of my soul
Of me, the essence of me
That thing that only I am, and only I can be
That thing that is not part of another world
That thing that is private
It gives me strength
And the power to move
That helps me to find the words inside of me
So that I may create something that everyone
Someday will say
Yes. That's me too.

Lost

When did I lose me?
The person who I am
Whoever that is
When did I lose the right to be private?
To have thoughts, dreams, live my way
They judge me, follow me and ask me why
They claim they know me
But they only know what I had to be
Not who I am.
They only know what they made me to be
But not who I was before them
When they look at me
They see someone old
Someone who struggled
Someone not worthy of respect
Someone who lived for them too much
They resist me trying to be free
Trying to get out of this cage
That responsibility has given me
That I lovingly accepted
What exists outside of who I have been?
And who I have yet to be
I need to find what makes my heart beat
My palms sweat
Something that definitely is me
Something that only I can do

Eraser of Self

Where is that person
That I am not yet
Who is that person in the mirror?
She looks back at me, but does she exist?
Does anyone else see themselves?

Lynn Larson Armstrong

Do they see me? The person behind the mask
Covered, hiding from the world
That tells me who I am
Living in compartments neatly organized
Mother
Wife
Aunt
Coworker
Lover
Fighter
Creator
Destroyer
Writer
Eraser of self

Pictures

I see pictures of me and I hate them. I used to think I would grow out of
me. Like I would become some beauty queen.
Someone on TV. I used to think my day will come soon, but
I never really changed. Now I see my girls, they are beautiful, but not sure of themselves. Did I do that?

Night Fear

Sometimes in the night

Suspicion grows
It seeps in through the window
And creeps along the floor
And underneath the bed
The silence begins to roar.

As you lay in bed it waits
And if you try to escape

Lest you jump beyond its reach
That beast will drag you underneath.

The heavens erupt, the angels cry
Their tears stream down your windows
While bolts of lightning pierce the sky
And through the tears you'll see it there
Waiting for you to close your eyes.

There's only one way to defeat the beast
That lies beneath your bed
That seeps in through your window
And creeps inside your head.

You must confront the demon
If you dare for unless you do
It will always be there.

Silly Me

I fell
To my knees
Let my feet go
Never good
Silly me
I slipped
Let them down
Silly me

Lynn Larson Armstrong

Look Away

Hold me close
Kiss me
Like I am beautiful

See my beauty
Not my scars
Like I was meant to be

Look away from me
Before you see me
Like I really am.

It's OK

There are times
When he was all she needed
When he would make her smile
And laugh when she would look at him
And know it was ok

Look inside my eyes and see my soul
Feel my joy understand my pain
Look inside my eyes and feel my heart

There was a time when there was no laughter
When he stopped looking back with smiling eyes
When his eyes went dark and he looked away
When the smile left his face
And she started to think, maybe it's not ok

Look inside my eyes and see my soul
Feel my joy understand my pain
Look inside my eyes and feel my heart

There is always a time
When this moment should pass

When there is no smile, no reassurance
When it's ok to know that not everything is always alright

Look into my eyes and see my soul.
Remember all the reasons
You loved me. And love me still.

Strength and Courage

When you give all that you have
And still it's not enough
When you come to the edge
One last time, and you take yet another step

When the hurt that you feel
Is hollow and aching in your heart
And your soul aches
Because you know it will never be the same

When you cry and you cry until there are no more tears
And still your eyes well up, one last time
When you hopes are destroyed
And you along with them and still you reach out

When there is no passion
And it seems the heart is all gone
When the words I love you
Are confused with the anger and the fear

When the words are not heard
Muddled by the noise within
When you just want to reach out and make the pain stop
But he just gets farther away

When you have to give up
Because he doesn't want to be loved and to love
You let go. One last time.
To live to heal and love again.

Lynn Larson Armstrong

Mine Only

Sometimes a particular sadness overcomes me
Out of nowhere it appears
Triggered by a memory, a loss, a loneliness
Drifting in without notice
An intruder that never really leaves
Reveals me to myself
All my regrets, my failures
My Heart sinks, breath slows
As I heed the intruder's message
Holding on to myself
Waiting humbly for its passing
For this is my penance
Mine alone to bear, never to share.

Saw you today.

Saw you today
Felt you walk by
But you didn't see me
You never looked back
You didn't feel me
You are lost to me.
Saw you today
But you didn`t see me.

Why she cries.

She looks in the mirror,
Turning first to the left and
Then to the right
Her eyes shift, they narrow
And focus
On a single eyebrow hair, a tiny mark on her check,

A childhood scar when she fell on the street.
She is beautiful. But not to him.

Eyeliner, mascara meticulously applied
She straightens her curly hair,
And pulls it back from her face
She puts on her best, and takes a deep breath
And turns to face what is hers alone
The fear of being alone
Of not being good enough
Of being told she doesn't measure up

That he doesn't love her anymore
That maybe he never did
She's afraid of the feeling that she will feel
When she realizes she's not good enough
When she knew she never was.

She cries for what could have been
For the wish that she had
For failing to break through his rock hard shell
For each time she wished she had said something different
Or done something else
For each time she was critical, impatient or wrong

No matter how hard she tried, she thinks
No matter how beautiful she was
No matter how much she loved him
And had been there for him
She failed

She imagines their life together,
What it could have been
And she loves him,
For all that he is, and all that he has yet to be.
She regrets that she will not see the person
She knows is inside of him

Lynn Larson Armstrong

Wondering what the world has lost
Because they lost each other.

She imagines the names of their children,
Will they have her eyes and his nose?
Will they be creative like her, and strong like him?
Will they be good parents, and grow old together?
She dreams.

Scared of being lost and alone
Of not having the life with him that she imagined
Of feeling rejected for the love that she gave
Of never being loved again by him
Of never living again
Of never being whole
Without him.

She is afraid to let go, to forget about him
Because then he will be gone
And she will be left with a hole in her heart
An aching pain in her chest
Where her heart was beating
The last time he touched her neck . . .
Kissed her goodbye

If only she could see what others see
A beautiful girl who was born that way
Someone strong, creative and loving
If she could see, she would not cry,

If she could only feel the strength
Those others feel when they are near
Amazed by her gifts that grow stronger
Each time she gives them away
In a sculpture, a painting, a word
A smile.

If she could only see what others see
But all she can see is what he does not
The love of her life that hurts so much

She hangs on for small gestures,
A wink, a nudge, a smile
To notice her hair, her eyes
Her kindness, her love for him
To hold her hand
And be proud to be near
To love and to be loved
That's all it would take.
And so she cries.

She Died.

Of a hard life lived she died
With a broken heart never loved
Too much pain to live
Too much heart ache
To endure, she died.
Wishing that things would get better
That mercy would find her
And save her from this dark place
That night would break and day would come
It did.
And now she lives

Obituary of a life unlived.

She was blond with green eyes
A shadow of who she should be.
What a shame.
She never knew who she could be
What she could do
What a shame she never felt

How she made me feel.
What a shame.

Part 2: Defiance

Purpose

A proud northern tree
Emerged from a fallen acorn
Imbedded in a rocky crack
Stretches out to feel the sun.

A free bird in flight
Wings stretched
Floating across the sky

A strong mountain
Crashing and heaving
From below the surface
Breaks through.

A child is born out of a wish and a dream.
To be proud. Free. To be strong.

Defiance

To do what others would not do
Disapprove of
To turn left instead of right
To do despite what others say
Wondering and not approving
Leaving me alone
Unable to carry on
Unable to look at me
Unable to fathom my defiance
Unwilling to understand

Not able to see what could have been seen
Only to judge
To nod in disgust.
I don't care.
I am defiant.

Free me.

Inhale life.
Run as fast as I can
Let each moment wash over me
Like a wave washes over the shore
Bask in the pain and the joy
Experience what it is to feel pain
To feel joy.
Ecstasy.

Opening

Open my ears to be filled with music
Fill my soul
With rhythm and joy
So that I may sing out loud.
Open my eyes
And show me the beauty
That surrounds me
So that I can see what I have never seen
With innocence and wonder
Free my body,
So that I can dance.

Lynn Larson Armstrong

Inked

The needle scrapes the skin
Carving a memory forever
A vision of mine
Of how I see myself
That feels like my heart beating
That captures my love
And my life
My need to be free
To give up control
But not lose control
To be open to new ideas
And to new experiences
Brought to life
By an artist
A stranger
In ink.

Answers

Living in the moment
Being hurt, frustrated, loved, happy
Motions of time
Seemingly unwinding the course of our lives
Not knowing how to get to the next place.

This collective journey of one
Stumbling and falling
Wishing and hoping there is a master plan
Complete with answers about why, where, when and how.

We speak upon deaf ears
In unison
To no one who listens for the sake of hearing
Who cares enough to not give answers

And I find myself screaming from the top of my lungs
It is not the answers that we give
It is the questions we must hear.

Just Human

To be the first person who fell
Under the force of the great mountain
That I once carried to protect you from the rain

Defeated, the tidal waves overcome me
The ocean's force that beat me against the rocks
Battered me, leaving me weak
With a punishing force
Without mercy, without care

Nothing left to do
But pick up the pieces
Find a way to be stronger next time

To admit to being human
Being wrong
To admit that finding my way
Took some turns and twists

To realize that everyone falters, every one fails, not just me.

I Cry

Sometimes I sit and cry
Tears of happiness
Tears of sadness
Remorse
Regret
Love
Loneliness

Lynn Larson Armstrong

The first time I said I do
To the one I love
The first time I felt a heart beat inside me
The first time I saw my baby's faces
The first time I choked back
My fears
And took a step anyway
The first time I broke the rules
The first time I wished I had
The last time
Was yesterday.

Ice Cracking

Ice cracking on a lake
Sounds like a door slamming
Thunder
Echoes across the ice
Once
Then again
Contagious
Spreading
To the end
Until it reaches the shore
It knows not when it will stop
Or how far it has to go
It only responds
To the pressure
Of the heat
Of the warmth
Of the need to break free
From the winter
To find the sun.

Those Times

Those are hard to forget
Memories that came in a flash
But never seem to leave

Memories that are fleeting
But are with me still
Left me in a place
Where I never was before
Where I was lost
And couldn't find my way

Where I discovered who I am
Who I can be
What else is inside of me?
That I never knew existed

I have since left that place
But not really
A part of me stays back there
Wondering if the rest of me
Will ever come back

Tidal Wave

The tide rushes in
Crashing against the rocks
Its back arches
Against the force of the stone
It succumbs
And falls backward
Into the sea
Only to rise again.

Search Light

I sit alone here in my watchtower
Listening to the waves heaving and crashing
And retreating back to the ocean
I wonder if anyone out there can hear me over the roar
Here alone on my watchtower.

Release Me

Pain in my chest
Shortness of breath
Deafens me.
Eyes closed, I imagine
Another time and place
Someone else
She is not me.
She is free, sensual.
She loves and loves
To be loved, not afraid,
Guilty or apologetic.
She moves freely
Without fear
Reaching out . . .
Not afraid to be touched
Pain in my chest
My heart beats
Furiously, bursting to be free

Deafening.
Pounding at the walls
My body of stone
That surrounds me
Protects me
Shortness of my breath
My voice screams

Deep from within my lungs
Where it has been trapped
For an eternity
Free me,
Reveal the person who I am
Whom I have not yet met
Afraid of being seen.
That's me.
Behaving, not speaking
Smiling.
Speaking only when spoken to
Release me.

Every Moment Reflection

Every moment is a life lived
A rare second that lives and dies in a flash
An experience that changes
That lasts a lifetime
The first kiss
The first time
The first smile
The first baby
The first tear that fell from love
The last time you said goodbye

Every moment is a life lost
A time that can never be come again
A word that can never be said
A kiss that can never be had
A touch that can never be felt
Memories that of wishing and would haves
Live forever and come forward from that past

Every moment is meant to be lived.
Moments of joy, passion, regret and sorrow

Meant to be experienced
That create the collection of a lifetime.

I Close My Eyes

I close my eyes
And think about the times
When I felt most alive
The times when I my heart was pounding
When my palms would sweat
When I couldn't catch my breath
When I could sigh
And it would come from deep down inside
Expelling the pain
Replenished with joy and passion
With love and being loved

I close my eyes
And look for the place where I am loved
Where I love
Where I feel joy
Where I am released from my wrongs
From my pain
From my loss

I close my eyes
And imagine a time that came unexpectedly
A time when I let go of my fears
Of my insecurity
Of a time when I felt beautiful and young, desired, alive
If I could go there again
I would in a minute.

There is a place

There is a place inside of me
That I wish you could reach
That I wish you could feel
That I wish I could feel

There is a place inside of me
A place that feels empty
A place that, when opened
I can never close again

There is a place inside of me
That you touched
Without meaning to
A place that you reached

When you spoke my name
When you looked into my eyes
When you brushed back my hair
When you kissed me goodbye

There is a place that must be left
Alone, not to share
Not to touch, never to be.

There is a place that I feel
Pulling at me
Reminding me of a time
A moment that came and passed

Speechless

What cannot be said in words, or thought out loud
That lingers through my mind searching for reason or rhyme
A story not yet written but stands the test of time
Plays on my mind, over and over

Perhaps this place is not mine to touch,
Not my story to tell, not my memory to live.
Still I search to touch what is beyond my grasp,
If only to be alive in that moment . . .
To utter those words if they did exist

Release a memory once silenced by logic,
Locked away for eternity, for duty and virtue
Beyond the poet's scope
This melody for which there can be no music.
This song for which there can be no words
This play for which there can be no stage

And I realize, at last, that I am powerless
Drawn to where words fail me
Where fate has shown me something
That I do not understand
A dream that is not real
Alive only in that place between night and day
Between now and then.
For the first time in my life
I realize
I am speechless.

OK in the moment

A life time of happiness
Is a vision
Of the human condition
To be happy, satisfied and content

To look back at the end and say
"That was good."

To live in each moment
Waiting for the next to begin
To be "balanced"
Is to be human, but not whole.
To live in all parts of one's life

To play each role
As if Shakespeare had written it himself
To find joy in the small moments
And see the gift that is each experience
A kiss, a hug, a tear, a loss
That is the life that I choose to live.

See me

See my beauty
Not my scars
Like I was meant to be
Look away from me
Before you see me
Like I really am.

Battered

Took a step today for I was not afraid
Wanted to see what was on the other side
How it feels to feel
To touch and be touched
To inhale and without care
Let go.
Bloody and battered
I hit the ground with a thud

Unforgiving and unrelenting
I took a step today and lived.

Compelled

Compelled I was unable to retract
And regain my ground
Compelled I was unable to escape
This place where I am.
Compelled I was to go there
To that place where
I have never been.

I thought

I thought I would be the one
To play with fire
To walk away
Without a thought.

I thought I would be the one
Who was sure of myself

I thought I would be the one
To see you fall
To cause your pain

I thought I would be the one
Who could not be touched
Who would not feel
But I was wrong.

Message in a bottle

I knew this would hurt
But I did it anyway
Jumped in
Got in way over my head
Drowned before I had a chance to get out.

When I think of it, it was already too late . . .
The first time you remembered things that I said
When I thought no one was listening.
The first touch of my hand
The first time I was able to take a breath
so deep,
As if waiting all my life to exhale.

If I could have seen to the end of that day
I would have kissed you more and worried less,
Trusted my feelings and stayed longer in your embrace.
Now that you are gone, I wish that I would have
Etched each word, every smile, every glance in my memory,
Stopped thinking in rhyme,
And said it out loud. "I love you."

I would have let you go gracefully,
Let you know that it's not your fault
That you tried to love me
That I was too afraid to stay
That you got caught in the wake of my change.

Still, I am helpless but to go where my feelings take me.
Like the sea that bends to its rock,
I am weak, yet craving more,
Cheated, yet fulfilled.

If I could, I would hold your hand
Pull you close to me.
Hear your heart beat next to mine.

Feel your breath,
Intertwined with mine.

Adrift, I wait
For this pain to subside
Wondering, if you think of me
If you ever looked back to find me
Entombed, I remain
Alone, waiting
To fall out love
For peace to find my soul.

CHAPTER 3:

On That Day, I Fell From The Sky
And Began To Fade To White

"Forget. Sounds good. Forgive. I am not sure I could. They say, time heals every-
thing, but I am still waiting. I am through with doubt. There's nothing left for me
to figure out. I've paid a price and I will keep paying. I am not ready to make nice.
I am not ready to back down. I am still mad as hell, and I don't have time to go
round and round and round. It's too late to make it right. I probably wouldn't if I
could. Cause I'm mad as hell, can't bring myself to do what it is you think I should.

Dixie Chicks, Not Ready to Make Nice

A flamingo fades to white

I met a flamingo who had temporarily lost the will to dance. I found her
afraid and lost, wandering and frustrated, trapped inside a cage of self -doubt
and questioning.

She was a successful flamingo, her resume of accomplishments well docu-
mented and well supported. She was a leader of compassion and vision. Her
resume of managing, manoeuvring and navigating the ponds of the ruling duck-
tators impressive. She had become adept at managing the most caustic of environments, and in fact, flourishing and stepping up when her duck counterparts
scattered for the weeds at the first sign of trouble.

The burden of this stress weighs heavily upon many of us who put all of our
energy into everything that we do, sometimes to our peril. In the throes of war,
we do not realize that we are holding ourselves captive when we stay too long.

Flamingos are not weak beings. We are the people who make things happen
by winning the support of others. So we are used to managing difficult situations, and in fact, we thrive in challenge. Each time, we tell ourselves we can

overcome and that everything will be alright. We are natural born leaders, who know how to lead, organize and inspire.

We terrify the disorganized, the despots and the disengaged because we are their antitheses, their nemesis. Flamingos are those to whom we go for advice and guidance because they create a safe environment. Flamingos look after their flock and protect them from predators.Flamingos are non-confrontational beings. People love us because we tend to smooth ruffled feathers.

As is often the case, our strength can be our weakness, and so we persevere when perhaps we should fly. When we stay too long, we lose our colour and our zest. We begin to question and doubt the very essence of who we are and why we have always been successful…and we take responsibility for the failures of others when we should let them stand alone.

When we are in the throes of doing battle we stop finding enjoyment in the little things that used to make us smile, because warriors don't smile. We lose our relationship with ourselves, and abuse our bodies with bad food and other vices in search of relief.

Our duck friends tend to scatter at the sound of trouble. Flamingos travel in flocks and are never alone. We take a running start before we fly, and when we take off, we can fly like none other.

Sometimes we stay too long on the runway, and we lose that which makes us strong – our colourful effervescence and our ability to dance. But a flamingo is a flamingo and never shall never a duck be. And when we find the music, we dance, a little wiser. When we fly, we paint the sky.

Making Deals and Pressing Smile

Every day the flamingo pushed the "smile" button on the elevator, hoping the storm would break. She made deals with herself, resolving to smile under the pressure that was building. She had been managing her job without adequate support and resources and it was taking a toll on her life. She told herself that they would never let them see they were hurting her. So she smiled, while the clouds built, and the rain kept coming. Risk was in the air. Each day was an exercise in faking it. She thought her dance performance was convincing.

Sometimes there were clashes between the creative thinkers – the artists, the writers and inventors – and the linear thinkers – the accountants, the project managers and the number crunchers.

This was not her first difficult duck. In the boardroom, she was trained and well versed in the language of brown ducks. In fact, she had come to appreciate the ways of the brown duck world, with their flow charts and spreadsheets.

She could empathize with the brown duck, dealing with a gregarious, outgoing, creative individual who seemed beyond their control. Many a flamingo has asked the question, "Why is the duck so uptight?" This conversation depicts the classic duck-flamingo difference.

Duck: "You are like a butterfly flitting from here to there. I can't catch you."

Flamingo: "Stop trying."

Awkward silence . . .

Duck <inside voice>: What?

Flamingo <inside voice>: I feel the micromanagement building. He is afraid that he won't know what he needs to know should the coffee conversation become strategic.

Flamingo: "Don't worry. I will set up a meeting every two weeks and keep you up to date on what's happening. You will always know what you need to know. I will never make you look bad."

Duck: "I appreciate that. Thank you".

The Rain of Nails Came Down

The air was so thick she could taste it. She told herself, "in six months everything will be better." Just as her strategy had worked in the past, there was every reason to believe this working relationship would improve. Somewhere, deep down inside that carefully selected suit and tie was the heart and soul of a duck-being, or perhaps a flamingo screaming for freedom.

This time communication was difficult and scant. Their work styles conflicted and conciliation or compromise seemed to be out of the question. The duck was directive and argumentative and attempted to overpower and over rule her. The flamingo, facilitative and conciliatory, would negotiate the terms of freedom on a day-by-day basis. Then one day, the rain of nails came down upon her behind closed doors and she fell from the sky.

"I acquired you," he began, "so the process today is going to be a different than what you expect."

Lynn Larson Armstrong

She immediately felt uneasy – like she had lost her footing. She became aware of the closed door and the fact that she was now a sitting duck; a flamingo without a flock. She was afraid.

The duck started by asking what her strengths were. Startled by this approach, she talked about the competencies that were relevant to her job performance trying to get the discussion back on track. She felt like a bird of prey was circling over her, waiting for an opportunity to attack.

"You are wrong," demanded the duck. "You should have given me one word answers rather than descriptions."

The duck accused the flamingo of having low self-awareness. This became the launch pad for his tirade, criticizing her both professionally and personally, saying she was ineffective with her time, that she was a poor communicator and that she talked too much. All the while the duck was reading from his document.

"What are you reading? Where is this?" she asked.

The duck sailed a document across the desk at her.

"I made some changes to yours. Use this one."

The words were there in black and white. She was horrified.

"You can't say these things in a corporate document!" she objected. "I will not accept the document with these words."

His phone rang repeatedly as she sobbed in anger. The duck answered each phone call, letting her know that she was truly disposable. She started to look for a way out.

"Who would believe this? Who could I tell, she wondered? Even if they believed me, would they support me? The door is closed. It would be the duck's word against mine."

She had to get out of that office with the document in hand. Her mind turned from outrage to strategy. As the phone rang incessantly, the duck had become impatient to leave. She asked the duck to send the document electronically and he did. She sent it home.

She went home that day, thinking she just needed a little time to regroup. His rat-a-tat voice hammered her memory. Despairing and hoping to stop the replay in her mind and help her to report the experience to…somebody, she wrote things down, verbatim,

Back safely in denial by the end of the weekend, she bought a new suit (of armour). It was a navy double-breasted pant suit. She readied herself to do battle or to appease the duck depending on the fallout and talked herself into returning to work like she had many times before.

She drove to work and pulled into her parking stall. The thought of coming face to face with the duck and having to relive the humiliation again was too much. She backed out never to return.

The Secret

In the work pond, there is a secret that many are keeping, bound and silenced by shame, fearful of speaking out, lest they suffer consequences of lost employment. This secret is what perpetuates the problem, protects irresponsible actions, prevents solutions and ultimately continues to condone bad behaviour in the workplace.

I feel compelled to address the issue of work place bullying in my own way, as I have the benefit of both experience and observations to share, and it was the final precipice upon which I decided to change the colour of the sky in my world.

Many people navigate bad work environments and bad behaviour for a pay cheque. Very few people speak out because there are consequences. We just hope these people will go away, or get promoted to someone else's pond. But there are consequences to silence and lack of acknowledgement of the problem and its impact on the person.

While the risk of being bullied is high, it is not so much the event that causes the damage as it is the secret. In the aftermath, there is fear, shame and a deafening silence followed by social distancing.

The risk of being bullied is high, as is the impact, say statistics. Anti-harassment policies have been established and measures are being taken, but still, the stigma of abuse weighs heavily on the victim. Telling the story is humiliating and often invites further retribution and abuse.

The issue of bullying is broadly discussed at the institutional and societal level. It is a problem, and a behaviour that is tolerated and excused despite the fact that we know it is a problem.

My theory is that people who treat others badly are badly mannered, fearful, insecure and poorly socialized with low emotional intelligence. When they become leaders, they can become dangerous.

I have observed that we make excuses for these poorly managed individuals, such as "they don't mean what they say", or "they are not that way once you get to know them", or my personal favourite, "he or she is just like that."

How it feels

It hurts because bullying is personally devastating. It affects the health and wellbeing of each and every one of us because we depend on our jobs for our livelihood at a bare minimum.

The workplace, like the pond, feeds and sustains us with status, a pay cheque, paid vacations, benefits, being part of a community, security and a sense of importance and purpose. We persevere during the difficult times because so much of ourselves is invested in our careers and the stability that we enjoy as a result. There is a saying that we join organizations and leave managers. Sometimes, we join an organization and hang on until the current manager moves on and another (better) one comes along.

Grief.

"So hard to move on, still loving what's gone. They say life carries on. Carries on and on, and on." – I Grieve, City of Angels by Peter Gabriel.

It feels bad to be abused, rejected, neglected and disrespected by someone who has power and control over you, no matter if you are a 10 year old child or an executive.

Shock, embarrassment, anger, shame and fear are your companions. In addition there have been casualties: trust, pride, dignity, security, self worth, professional status, social status, and personal well being.

In my research, the best description that I could find matching how it felt to me is that of a person affected by Post Traumatic Stress Disorder.

Aside from the emotional ride that ensues, there is a grieving process that we undergo when we lose something or someone, such as the loss of one's status, dignity, source of income, community and time spent in our lives that we dedicate to building a career.

This is a mourning process because a loss has occurred. There are five stages of normal grief. They were first proposed by Elsabeth Kubler-Ross in her 1969 book *On Death and Dying*.

Many people do not experience the stages in the order listed below, she says. The key to understanding the stages is not to feel like one must go through every one of them, in precise order. Instead, it's more helpful to look at them as guides in the grieving process — it helps the person understand and put into context where he or she is.

Denial and Isolation

The first reaction is to deny the reality of the situation. It is a normal reaction to rationalize overwhelming emotions. It is a defence mechanism that buffers the immediate shock. I wanted to block out the words and hide from the facts. This temporary response carried me through the first wave of pain.

I isolated myself from my friends and family. I disassociated with all things related to my work, blocking people from contacting me in various ways. I stayed home for four months, embarrassed and ashamed that this had happened to me. I kept the secret from friends and family outside of my husband and close friends who had been experiencing a similar situation.

In situations where I was forced to venture out, I was afraid of seeing someone from the work environment. I would scope out malls and stores, and when I did see them, I would pretend that I did not know them.

Denial helped me to manage the short bursts of time that I had no choice but to venture out of my home, such as going to the gym and non-profit work, when I would have to keep the secret of what was happening to me.

Anger

As the masking effects of denial and isolation begin to wear, reality and its pain re-emerges. The intense emotion is deflected from our vulnerable core, redirected and expressed instead as anger. The anger may be aimed at inanimate objects, complete strangers, friends, family, or oneself. We feel guilty for being angry, and this makes us angrier.

I would find myself becoming angry when things or people reminded me of the day the rain of nails came down. I became angry that my finances had been interrupted and that I was forced to retreat socially. I was angry that this secret kept me from living my life. I was angry that this story was alive in my memory, and that there was no indication of it becoming a fading memory.

Bargaining

The normal reaction to feelings of helplessness and vulnerability is often a need to regain control. I told myself that things would get better with time. I even set timelines. "In six months this will be a bad memory." I told myself that they were not aware of the impact of their actions, and that once they knew, everything would be better. I was hoping something would break - that this was just a big misunderstanding that I could return, that there would be an apology or acknowledgement. I wanted my life back as it was, rain and all.

Depression

I felt sadness and regret, worried about the financial costs, and whether or not I would ever work again. I painted my way through the feelings, changing the colour of the walls in my house, inside and out. I ventured out only to buy more paint, and I painted the feelings away under the sun. The walls of my home were transformed from dark rich shades of red, gold, purple and grey to a palette of whites. I was searching for the light.

Acceptance

Reaching this stage is a gift not afforded to everyone says Kubler-Ross. When something is sudden and unexpected we may never see beyond our anger or denial. It is not necessarily a mark of bravery to resist the inevitable and to deny ourselves the opportunity to make our peace. This phase is marked by withdrawal and calm.

I wanted acceptance more than anything. I wanted to move forward. I did not want this careless moment to define me. I wanted my life back. Before letting go, there was a final realization that that there was no going back. That it was over, and that I had no choice but to let it go. That there would be no phone calls, no bargains, no apologies. A new day would come and it did. On the day of emancipation, I wore gold shoes.

CHAPTER 4:
Some Grounding Thoughts on Flying

Lessons in Downward Facing Dog

I remember one night in a Level 3 Yoga Class, our teacher instructed us to find a Downward Facing Dog (Adho Mukha Svanasana) with wood blocks under both hands and feet.

Downward Facing Dog is a precarious position to begin with. It is an inverted pyramid shaped, face down position. With my hands and feet perched on blocks, I teetered on the edge of pain, fear of falling, and the certain humiliation that would follow.

In the first wave, I adjusted my body and weight, attempting to keep the blocks from sliding off my mat, so that I could avoid an embarrassing belly flop right onto my mat. In the next wave, my hands and feet began to hurt.

My legs were vibrating and my shoulders shaking. In the third wave, I became an observer of my own experience, noticing how interesting the pain had become. I had somehow left my body, in order to escape the pain of the moment. When I was finally able to dismount from my blocks (very carefully executing my best *Cirque du Soleil* dismount), my teacher said with a smile on his face, "We never hold that shit long enough."

When something hurts, we often focus first on how it feels. We try to manage it so we can avoid feeling the pain. At some point, if the pain persists, we become angry by the fact that we are hurting. We still want to avoid the pain, so we dip in and out of denial, telling ourselves all manner of lies and justifications. At some point, if we are lucky, we accept the pain, appreciate it in the moment as a gift, and find the lesson to be learned. That's the hard part.

Finding Balance

Through my years of working long hours to prove myself and taking on mammoth projects, I always felt like I was not keeping up in the parts of my life where I was not getting a pay cheque. I told myself it was necessary to support my family. I also felt like it was necessary to continue growing in my career. My New Year`s resolutions usually including getting balance into my life.

Looking back now, I had no idea what it meant or how to achieve it. I could not visualize what it meant to have balance so how was I ever going to attain it. During `The Belly of the Great Whale` time, I began a dedicated practice of yoga. At first I was looking to release the negative energy of work and life. Over time, I became aware of movement, breath and grounding. I began to visualize what balance looked like, and felt like.

Balancing on one foot in a Tree Pose for example, requires that the standing foot is rooted in all four corners of the foot. Energy travels upward from there, lifting the knee cap, thigh muscles and into the rib cage. Hips are evenly balanced across the body, as are the shoulders. On the mat, in order to achieve balance, we are constantly in a state of grounding and lifting, pushing and pulling and contracting and expanding.

This is true off the mat as well. In order to find balance, it is important to understand that balance is also about being aware of what we give and take, and what we are holding on to and letting go of.

Holding on to something is easy, because it is something that we hold near and dear. We hold on to our values, our principles and our beliefs because these are part of our self-constructed world view. We are usually holding on to something because it has some emotional attachment for us, like religious beliefs, or even a teacup that belonged to a family member.

Letting go is difficult because it requires dismantling the reasons for holding on. Letting go of beliefs that no longer serve us changes our world view. Sometimes it is inconvenient to change, even if it`s for the better. Letting go of a tea cup can represent letting go of a person. Letting go of a habit, like smoking for example, means letting go of something you have come to know and trust, even if it is damaging.

In the strategic planning realm, where I have facilitated mergers, I have observed that invisible attachments may be present in the room that prevent moving forward. We need to clean out the closet of our lives, and determine

Lynn Larson Armstrong

what to keep and what to toss in order to make room for more. Here are some items worth considering if you are planning to fly someday.

Abdication versus Engagement

When I was a corporate planner early in my career, I could see how powerful it would be if the people who came to work every day actually believed in what they were working for. With that in mind, I created and implemented planning systems that would inspire people to commit more of themselves to their work or employer. I remember describing it as *bringing themselves to work*. I thought that if a person brought even 80% of himself or herself to work, and if everyone was able to do that, the organization would be successful beyond all measure. Some organizations have been able to achieve this, at least for a time, but not all organizations deserve this level of loyalty.

I gave of myself passionately and freely to my work and to my employers. I was a stellar employee every day. My children can attest to the hours that I spent working, even at home, right up until the day I backed out of my parking stall.

During my years as a strategic planner, we would measure employee satisfaction annually. Loss of personal control is one of the greatest stress factors. When we feel like we are not in control of our destiny, we begin to feel nervous because at that point, we become vulnerable, like a sitting duck, or a flamingo without a flock. When you combine the loss of personal control with a culture that does not inspire trust, the result is a very bad work experience for the employee and very likely and deservedly poor performance for the company.

From a personal standpoint, there is a fine balance between doing a good job to build a positive reputation and abdicating and relinquishing control to another.

The air gets fuzzy when time, money, reputations and status are at stake. Even though I could see how important it would be to inspire people to engage, the further up the mountain I travelled in my work, the more uninspiring it became.

At the peak of the mountain, there were times when I made deals with myself, hoping to persevere for my pay cheque, like many of us do when we find ourselves at the precipice. I saw the signs that a storm was building, but I rolled the dice and hoped for sunny days.

Eventually I left, but not everyone does. To those still teetering on the precipice, I would say, be healthy, do some yoga, have interests outside of work that are not dependent on work, let work be work and breathe, because without oxygen you will suffocate.

Who I think I am

Loss of identity is one of the reasons that we stay too long. We forget that we are not the job that we do. We believe that we are defined by and receive status from the job that we do, or the title on our business card, or the pay cheque that we receive. The day that I fell from the sky and began to fade to white, I felt like I had lost something I had worked so hard to build and nurture. My job title had become my identity. When I decided not to return to that world, that part of my identity was gone as if it never existed. As if I had never been there. I became, for all intents and purposes, invisible and irrelevant, with the stroke of my own pen, to that world. At first, I felt as if I had been eradicated from the world to which I gave over 20 years of myself to build, but then I realized the sun would rise and it did.

I began this book with the question, who do I think I am, because I truly had to begin there again in order to begin again. I had to rethink about the concept of identity, unattached from the roles and titles that say something about what we do, but not who we are. The answer to the question, who do I think I am, is a mystery to me some days. I do know that I am bigger than a business card. I am how I show up in the world, and so I try to focus on showing up in a good way and helping to make a difference in the lives of others with the gifts that I have to offer.

Be an observer in your own story.

Writing is my way of quieting my mind and making sense of the world. In the course of learning to fly again, I attempted my write myself to freedom, to find the words that would set the story and me free once and for all. I wrote every single day about the story that changed my life and caused me to question myself on all levels. I spent more than one year writing my way to freedom.

Writing my way through this retrospectively was like being perched on blocks in a Downward Facing Dog for 15 painful minutes. The more I wrote, the more I experienced what happened, the more questions I had. How could this happen to me? Why did I let it happen to me? Why does this story have no end? What is it that I am supposed to be learning from this experience? Why can't I just let myself fall? What can't I just pretend this never happened?

The more I wrote, the more I could see my part in the story, the more I began to take back control of my own life and story. I had become an observer in my own story, a perspective which helped me to finally put the story to bed.

The perils of flying in reverse

As an observer, I could see that my perspective was holding me back from moving forward. I thought it was the crescendo of my career; the day the bodacious lady sang, (to upgrade a poorly articulated cultural euphemism that should be banished from language.) It was not the crescendo after all. It was the opportunity to move forward, and take with me what serves my life and leave behind the beliefs that had become blinders.

It was the day that I discovered that people, regardless of their titles or pay cheques, are human, and that we are each capable of less than noble or heroic deeds, and that we choose our actions consciously, so we are accountable. It was the day that would lead me to the place that I was yet to be, the place that was waiting for me.

We can only fly forward. The key to flying again is to stop telling the stories of the past, and discover the new world for the first time again.

A Living Intention

Beneath the blue sky and the vision, flows the river of intention that leads to all things good and bad. When it is filled with the best intentions and actions, it is good. When it is bad, it is just stinky. When it comes to intention, a leader's visions and intentions must be articulated, demonstrated and upheld at all costs.

Intentions are like mirrors. One of my mentors used to say, 'You are what you do'. In other words, nothing is an accident; each action is telling of who we are and our intentions.

In business, intention is a powerful statement that creates clarity about the future, focus on what matters, and a method to get the ducks in a row. Intention comes to life in culture and treatment of people, especially. In the corporate world, most employees do not participate in the creation of intention, nor do they see the words. But they feel it in their work experience and in the actions of their leaders. Good intentions without actions are just pretty words if there is no one who truly believes or champions the cause.

A living intention is different because it is personal. It inspires actions that create the stories of our lives in the present tense. A living intention permeates our being. It is part of the answer to the question, *who do I think I am*, because it is how I show up in the world.

Establishing intention takes some soul searching and awareness. It is a question of the heart, and not the mind. It requires culling the old stories and legends that we have acquired, but not necessarily chosen.

Do Good Things

I think it is apparent that people who have a positive impact on others have good intentions. These are the people who become the leaders and visionaries of our time. These are the people who we follow and look up to for answers. They are natural born leaders, not because of their title or pay cheque, but because of their intentions and their deeds. We look to people like Nelson Mandela, Mother Teresa, Steve Jobs and John Lennon but there are good people with good intentions who walk among us every day, true heroes who do good things and give of themselves to make a difference. These are the people who inspire me.

I have been very lucky to have walked beside some great people who do great things.

When I had the opportunity to recreate the life that I wanted, to live a life that I have chosen and not acquired by accident or circumstance out of duty or status, I saw it as a second chance to do good things that feel good to do, to love what I do and do what I do with love, to follow what I am passionate about and be nothing less than impassioned every single day of my life.

My mantra is to do good things so that good things happen. I say these words to myself every day both as a guiding intention in my business and my personal life.

CHAPTER 5:
The Flamingo's Guide to Flying

Sometimes we stay too long on the runway, and we lose that which makes us strong – our colourful effervescence and our ability to dance. But a flamingo is a flamingo and never shall never a duck be. And when we find the music, we dance, a little wiser. When we fly, we paint the sky.

Reflections in the Pond

I have no regrets. I have been very fortunate in my life to have worked with purpose. I have had the privilege of working with some great and memorable leaders who created not only positive, healthy organizations, but also legacies. The leader shapes the work experience for each employee, regardless of the size of company because the leader sets the pace for how an organization behaves, what it focuses on, and how people are treated. I have learned that going to work is an act of faith in the leader, so the quality of people in these high places matters. Here is what I learned in a nutshell about the leader's job:

> Leaders paint the sky, share the vision of what's possible, and
> inspire people to follow. Those who cannot are not.

Since Nirvana, I have always known what I needed to do: help people to articulate and realize their vision and do good things. I have held true to these intentions during the good times and especially during the times of challenge and change.

One person who worked alongside me during the Belly of the Great Whale era shared this thought with me:

> We learned a lot more during that period of time than a
> person normally does. Difficult circumstances can be a great

teacher, if you have the right perspective and leadership. My career is where it is at today because of the chance you took on me 10 years ago. And then all the stuff I learned from you. So thank you Lynn.

I would like to thank the people who took a chance on me, who did not fire me when I stood up in front of them in black leather pants with my vision of *Lynear Thinking* blasting, who shared with me their knowledge and insight and who continue to be my mentors today, even through the process of writing this story. I would like to thank the people who stood with me and behind me during the challenging times, giving me the strength to stand up and the courage to start again. I would like to thank my teachers who presented these life lessons to me so that I could carry forward what I have learned so that others may benefit too.

In my decision to venture into the world of entrepreneurship, here are the lessons that I carried forward that have proven themselves over and over again.

10 Lessons Learned

Lesson 1: Trust the CEO.

At Queen's University, we were asked to bring a management dilemma. Mine was navigating a post-merger environment with a challenging duck boss. On the first day, I was star struck by the people in the room. I was among some of the best and brightest minds in the country, at least according to their employers. As I scanned the room, my eyes fell on a man at the far end of the theatre. He was the most *CEO-est* looking person I had ever seen. With his perfectly chiseled demeanour and his calm and quiet stature, he struck me as a person who was not afraid of heights, who was accustomed to flying at high altitudes as the greatest leaders do.

As luck would have it, we ended up in the same working team. He was the vice president of a large grocery store chain. The management dilemma that he brought forward was what to do when one of the executives appears to be running counter to the CEO's direction. My job was to coach him on his dilemma. I looked up his company's quarterly results and could see the problem.

As I shared my advice with him, he said that I was accurate in my understanding of the issue.

During the course of our discussion, he said something that I have carried with me every day since: "Trust the CEO". In other words, support the CEO and trust that he or she will see the issue and address it in the best interests of the organization.

This piece of advice has served me time and time again in my career as a strategic planner for companies navigating challenging merger environments and ego-centric executives who sometimes believed in their own vision as opposed to that of the CEO.

From my seat at the table, I could see that the CEO provided that vision both through words and deeds. When the CEO retreats, so do his or her followers. A leaderless organization quickly becomes rudderless.

Trust is a fine balance. It must be earned, not decreed. The days of "do as I say because I say so" are over. I held strong to the belief that people, especially those who would call themselves a leader, rise to the challenge when they are trusted to do so.

Lesson 2: Tell the truth with courage, conviction, clarity and compassion.

I remember opening the front cover of a national bank annual report that had just been denied a merger with another financial institution. The copy, roughly paraphrased, said "our merger was denied, but we know we need to continue to find ways to achieve our goals and deliver shareholder value. This report is about how we will do that."

I was impressed because I could fully appreciate the courage that it took to publicly admit to failure and then focus on the way ahead.

The truth writes itself every time. As a corporate planner and writer, I have spent many an hour wordsmithing around the truth over the past 20 years. Good leaders are those who communicate with courage, conviction, clarity, truth and compassion. They confront the issues, and face the music when they are wrong.

Lesson 3: Create an environment where people can be successful.

Bees need to buzz. Ducks need to quack. Flowers need to bloom. Flamingos need to dance. People need to know how to contribute in a tangible way. Alignment is a corporate term that means "getting your ducks in a row" which means to ensure that all of the small details or elements are accounted for and in their proper positions. When a person is fully prepared for any eventuality and has every element in place, he or she can indeed be said to have his or her ducks in a row.

Lesson 4: Be respectful towards people and they might not organize a mutiny.

Communicating vision with clarity is all about the audience, the listener and understanding their perspective. Some, like the flamingos, prefer their vision served in broad brush strokes, and then there are the detail-loving brown ducks who want to know why, when, where, how and how much time and money will be needed.

Both perspectives are valid and important, especially when communicating sensitive issues like directional shifts, job changes, and re-organizations. The leader is the voice of clarity. He or she must therefore understand the needs of their flock, and be compassionate, fair, and factual.

Lesson 5: Be a CEO in your own life and stop waiting for someone else to step up to your plate.

Be a person. The best people with whom I have worked are those who care about their own development and who are not afraid to live in their own colours, be they pink or brown. The best employers care about the development of their people and make it a priority. Good employees do not abdicate their life to their employer. Abdication of one's personal potential, respect and time to anyone or anything is the first step in losing control over one's own destiny and a terrible price to pay for a job. What we do with our life and our talent is up to us. Work is merely an output of talent in a tangible form for a limited purpose. An employer does not owe its employees happiness. Happiness is an outlook. We make decisions about where we will work, why, and for how long. There are three choices, each bearing their own consequences: stay and work to make it better; accept the limitations (maybe what you want is not possible); or leave. But either way, be clear about your decision.

Lesson 6: Put your money where your values are.

In journalism school, one of my professors told us to "follow the money" when researching a story. The same is true for understanding the true values of the organization, how an organization is performing and how effective the leaders are in leading and inspiring their employees.

I found that money always follows the priorities of the leadership and that leaders who follow money exclusively are the least effective leaders. Financial outcomes are important in business. It is important to recognize that the way people are treated, including employees and customers, is an important part of what creates the financial results.

Where culture and treatment of people are strategic priorities of the company, financial resources are provided to attract and retain skilled people. By contrast, an organization where financial or political priorities outweigh others, efficiency and non-human investments become the priority. When one perspective becomes too important, the others suffer.

Lesson 7: Be Trustworthy.

Trust is earned every day. When we put ourselves in the hands of someone else every day, we need to know that we can trust that person. So leadership bears a great responsibility for trust. It is demonstrated in the way people are treated, the communication process, and the performance management process. It stands to reason that employees with a high employee engagement level have a high level of trust in the leadership and culture, and organizations with a low employee engagement level demonstrate low levels of trust in the leadership and culture.

Trust is especially important in engaging for performance. After all, if we do not believe that the person sitting across the table from us is honourable and trustworthy, why would we engage?

That is in essence what happens when an organization's leaders lose the trust of their flock. We disengage and pull back to protect ourselves.

Collectively if trust levels are low, the organization suffers and never fully utilizes the full potential of its workforce.

Sometimes, organizations with low engagement try to fix the problem with tactical responses, such as lunchrooms and recognition pins, but unless the core issue of trust is addressed, the problem will persist and grow to affect turnover rates, medical costs and legal costs, in addition to lost potential and productivity.

Consider the role that trust plays in a performance review where a person's livelihood and personal wellbeing is at stake, or in a change management process, where jobs are changing and people's lives are being altered.

Lesson 8: Listen to what people say about you.

Having worked for organizations with varying levels of employee satisfaction, from below 50 per cent to over 80 per cent, creating an inspiring place to work must begin with an intention at the top. When employee satisfaction is low, it is not hard to imagine that statistically speaking, many things need to be addressed – that everything is quite likely a little or a lot broken.

If leadership and management are defined as guiding the way to a positive strategic future, an abysmal and ongoing employee satisfaction rating is an indicator that leadership is ineffective.

Lesson 9: Measure what Matters

Setting measures is the first step in knowing what to focus on. Measures are indicators that tell the business owner what is happening. Measures are used to test the strategy so that ducks can check the wind direction and see if they are a still on course. Strategies can take a long time to prove themselves, so patience, thoughtfulness, honesty and integrity need to come to the table.

The question is inevitably asked: What to do when a number isn't quite cutting it on the corporate scorecard? Here are three possible responses.
   A. Question the environment and the strategy to determine
      what changes are required to get back on course.
   B. Question the tactics. Are we doing the right things?
      Is there an adjustment to be made?
   C. Question the measure and change it, hoping for a better outcome.
   The answer is A or B. But C gets picked sometimes, and here's why.

Lynn Larson Armstrong

When numbers are good, it generally follows that rewards and recognition are good. Organizations cheer about their success and write news releases and publish the good news where everyone can see it. If you are looking for a job, these tend to be the most attractive employers because chances are, they are doing a lot of good things and talking about it.

But when an organization is under performing on their measures, the information is downplayed with justification should someone find the information.

Having less than stellar numbers is not the end of the world but it might feel like that on a year-end bonus. It is an opportunity to make changes.

The CEO who leads a company wide effort to engage employees in finding solutions will be more successful than the CEO who does not.

The bottom line is this: A company with a long-term trend of upward movement is demonstrating leadership in addressing issues and engaging people in finding solutions. A company that has a long-term trend of minimal or downward movement is demonstrating a lack of ability to make change.

Lesson 10: Accountability begins at the top, where the decisions are made.

Having seen, experienced and led people in change through mergers, joint ventures, restructures and various other evolutions, I have great respect for the importance of good governance and oversight.

It is well understood in today's work world that healthy leadership practices create healthy work environments, as there is a direct correlation to increased employee satisfaction, productivity, and ability to retain and attract employees. Therefore, employee experience must be a strategic imperative for the Board of Directors, Owners and Shareholders.

The board's responsibility is to ask questions and not just receive answers, but to set the bar and hold its CEO to the bar through performance management. Sometimes, boards can be too passive in this regard, especially if their orientation is toward the numbers and not the people who create the numbers. Sometimes boards take action and replace the leadership. Sometimes their hands are tied. Sometimes they just don't have the information they need.

CHAPTER 6:
The Perfect Shade Of Possibility

What would I do if I could not fail? I would publish stories that are read world-wide about interesting and inspiring people who live and work in their passion. I would be an instigator of personal freedom. I would inspire people to accept and live in their own vision, and be inspirational to others to do the same. I would publish the book that changes the way we look at work. I would inspire a revolution of living in colour. I would paint the sky all the colours of possibility.

Finding What I Was Looking For

"I have been back to the place I had never been before; it was there that I realized I had been there all along. The way I see it, some people stand and look at the sky, others reach out and touch it." - Lynn Armstrong, Lynear Thinking

A mere 15 years after its debut at the Blue Sky session (where I presented, in black leather pants, my vision of *Lynear Thinking* to executives, with Bon Jovi`s 'Its my life' blasting) in 2011, I started my own company – *Lynear Thinking Strategy & Communications Consulting Ltd.* My clients are entrepreneurs, cooperatives and non-profits. In 2012, I bought *SKY Magazine*, a five year old quarterly publication.

Although I learned to quack and waddle convincingly in the corporate world for some 20 years, I knew nothing about the world of the entrepreneur, even though I was on the journey toward becoming an entrepreneur from the beginning.

There are distinct differences between the corporate world and the business world. In the corporate world, dollars and cents are really just indicators of success. In the entrepreneur's world, dollars and cents are deal breakers.

In the corporate world, the consequences of poor customer satisfaction are not directly and immediately linked to the bottom line. In the entrepreneur's world, customer satisfaction is the bottom line because it is the difference between making the sale or not.

In the corporate world, employee satisfaction and development are again distant indicators of a company's success or failure. In the private sector world, employee satisfaction and development have an immediate effect on the customer's buying decision.

Through *SKY Magazine* and *Lynear Thinking*, I help my clients connect to their employees, their shareholders, owners, stakeholders and their customers. Every day I find what I am looking for in the stories of the entrepreneurs who love what they do and take pride in how they do it.

Living close to the entrepreneurial ledge, I see time and time again those who are successful show integrity, take care of business and treat their customers and employees with the utmost respect. Those that don't are not successful. This is the world that I set out to discover. I have found the entrepreneurs, and they are us: living in full colour and dancing to their own heart beat.

Flamingo Project: Inspiring a Revolution of Living in Colour

Flamingos are community types. We have a gregarious nature and we love to party. In the wild, flamingos gather in large flocks. This serves to protect them from their predators - large vulture-like birds - that can swoop down and take their young. Flamingos need a long runway, but when they do fly, they paint the sky.

I launched the Flamingo Project as a blog when I started this journey of finding what I was looking for, which ultimately is the answer to the question, "Who do I think I am?" I often test what I am thinking there to get a public reaction.

Writing this story has been a journey. There are heroes and heroines and villains, like any good story. Many times along the way I stopped writing because sifting through the clutter was too much. In a blog post, I asked the question, who do I think I am to write and tell this story? A reader replied:

Who are you to tell this story? Who else?

You aren't likely the first to have been clipped and silenced and shattered in that world of remorseless unaccountability. And hopefully not the first to emerge in more vibrant colour and vocals. Fortunately you were and are a writer, and processed through journaling especially and then, the changing of 'persons' in the book. I wonder would the wounds just fester and not know how to heal in those without that outlet.

Easier to "back down & make nice". Safety matters - for sure. The first to find the courage, take the risks, tell the story...

That will be you
Why you
because you can
When it's time

One of my life goals was to teach yoga, so I applied and was accepted to a year long, 300 hour program. I have now completed it and am teaching yoga in my community. I only know that the more I learn, the more I need to know.

During my journey, both practicing and teaching has helped inform my perspective and my choices.

Yoga has a connecting quality. We are all connected through our experiences, our hopes, dreams and goals, and we are not alone. Yoga also means to settle the turmoil in the mind and body and disconnect the experiences from the individual to find a state of mindful awareness.

In a yoga class, I never feel the need to be noticed. I never feel like I have to bring something special to the group in order to belong. I never feel like a flamingo without a flock. Quite often, I practice with my eyes closed, guided by the sensation of movement and the sound of my teacher's voice.

One of my yoga teachers often says, "check and check again" when we are in a pose. She says, if you don't check where your hands and feet are, how will you know?

This works in Downward Facing Dog and in life. It is the practice of being aware and being in the moment. Finding my way back to me and learning to live in colour – in my own purpose - has been a process of renewal, rebuilding, and reinvention.

My yoga practice – the practice of maintaining a healthy connection to purpose and practice – has carried me through, and brought me face to face with my ego, my doubts, and fears and helped me to find success in the choices that I have made to live in colour.

Truthfully, all experiences are good but there are times when we need to stand up and stand out. I still believe people are inherently good. I believe that there is always a healthy way to resolve an issue without attacking someone. I believe things work out in the end regardless of how they feel in the moment. I also believe that people act out their intention, both good and bad purposefully and mindfully.

In the process of finding my yoga, I found a community that is beyond the scope of time and place. This community does not have an agenda, nor is it impressed by anything that I can do or bring. This community is one that is older than time and larger than any one person. There are common values, a language and principles, but these are not imposed, they are lived. The practitioner can take whatever he or she likes from it, and leave the rest behind, and still be accepted.

In my quest to find a place to belong, instead I found a place that just accepts me for who I am, so that I have the space to explore whatever that means.

In the course of writing this book and reflecting on the experiences, I used the practice of yoga to help me find the balance between holding on and letting go. There is no doubt that I was shaken to the core on that day that I fell from the sky. My life has changed for the better I believe.

I am sensitive to bullying, and I can no longer look away. I believe that we each have a responsibility to make the environment safe for each other. I strongly believe that if this were to be acted upon, bad behaviour would not be tolerated in person, at work, through social media or in any other way.

Here are some things that I try to remember to stay grounded.

1. Values and the Moving Train

I learned that values are uncompromising. In strategic planning sessions, I always say values are something for which one would stand in front of a moving train. This experience brought me face to face with my values and the moving train.

2. Practice Forgiveness

I say practice, because it doesn't come easy. Forget, maybe until you remember, and then the moment flares up as if it is happening. Forgiveness is the only way to subside the effects. Forgiveness is cathartic because it makes room for learning and insight, and that feels better than 1000 days of being angry.

3. "If you can't say something nice, don't say anything at all." -Thumper

When I was a child, we would listen to the story of Bambi at bedtime, and I always remember the words, "if you can't say something nice, don't say anything at all." As a writer and communicator, I am sensitive to the importance of words and how they affect people. We live in sensitive times and the right words are important and yet they flow abundantly and haphazardly. Words can heal. But they can also hurt. Words that are spoken are different from words that are written. Spoken words can run like water off a duck's back. Written words become records. Please be mindful of the words that we choose, and how they might affect others. And when all else fails, if you don't have something nice to say, don't say anything at all.

Lynn Larson Armstrong

The Colour of the SKY in My World

The thread that joins us is the belief in the endless horizon of possibility and the desire to reach out and touch it.

I was driving out to meet a client two hours away. The road was clear and dry. It was a cold winter's day here in the land under the sun at minus 27 degrees Celsius.

The sky was the perfect shade of ice blue, with wisps of white streaks occasionally drifting through.

As I looked out upon the prairie horizon, I could see perfect fields of white with tips of gold stubble peaking through. There was not a footprint in sight, as it was too cold for the wildlife.

I realized that day how far I had come. Up until 2011, I barely remember the colour of the sky on any given day. I don't remember what the sky looked like on the day I was married, or the day my daughters were born. Now I look up every day, and not only see the sky, but also how it connects to the land, and how it sustains and connects us.

I am grateful for these experiences because now I see not only the horizon, but I can reach out and touch it.

The End and the Beginning.

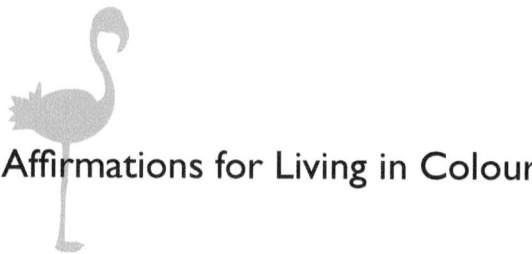

Affirmations for Living in Colour

Practice defiance three times a day

Stand up for things that matter and speak out against what is wrong or hurtful to others. Be courageous and persevere with an unwavering focus. Fill your life with family, friends, passions and interests, and if you are lucky, work is integrated. If not, do not let work define you. Define yourself by who you are inside and not what you do. If you do not know who you are, take some time to find out who you think you are.

Be imperfect and ever changing

Perfectionism is not a quality, and perfectionism does not lead to quality. It is the big brother of fear and insecurity and the killer of inspiration and creativity. Ditch the ego by learning humility and learning to stand on your hands. The act of falling over repeatedly is not only sure to bruise your ego, but likely to beat it to a pulp.

Listen and seek to understand

Be enthusiastic and positive. Keep good company and listen beyond the words to the intention of what is being said. Don't take it personally if they are not adept communicators. Give them the benefit of the doubt that they are unaware of the impact they are having by their words and actions.

Avoid rooms with no doors

Loss of personal control is one of the greatest stressors in life, which explains why people chose the exit sign as often as they do. Being trapped is a choice. I discovered that we create our own doors through the intentions we set and the values we model. We can also open doors for others by understanding their goals and aspirations. In case of emergencies, however, I also recommend carrying a reciprocating power saw with you at all times, should you need to create a door.

Do good things and good things happen

Help somebody. Help your community. Be helpful. Good karma follows good actions. Bad karma does too.

Thank you

I would like to offer my heartfelt thanks to my family, Mervin, Caitlyn and Sara who supported me through changing the colour of the sky.

I would also like to thank my teachers who helped me to make the connection back to the source of awareness, instead of the source of pain.